VILLAGES of ENGLAND

TIGER BOOKS INTERNATIONAL
LONDON

1374
This edition published in 1993 by Tiger Books International PLC, London
© 1987 Coombe Books
Printed and bound in Hong Kong
ISBN 1-85501-124-7

The village is one of the dearest aspects of English life. It can be found in no other country, though farming communities abound, and has grown steadily with the English people, not created by some civic planner. The beginnings of the village can be traced back to the days when the Anglo-Saxons came across the North Sea to settle in the decaying Roman Province of Britain.

At the time Britain was a wild and lawless place and the settlers soon learnt that isolated farms were easy pickings for bandits. It was found that a collection of farms was far safer. At the same time the then rather primitive level of agriculture meant that many farms couldn't be grouped together as the land could not support them. These two conflicting pressures dictated the development of the village as the basic rural community of the English. Though this made the settlers safe from bandits, it also made them tempting targets for larger war bands eager for pillage and plunder. In an attempt to avoid this fate the early Anglo-Saxon settlers created one of the main features of modern English villages; they are rarely on a main road. Invading armies were unlikely to know the area, so a hidden village was a safe village.

The coming of Christianity had a further influence. A new centre of the village was created when churches began to appear with the new religion. Understandably enough, most Anglo-Saxon churches have long since vanished but later churches were often built on Anglo-Saxon sites and can still be traced.

Many churches have been built on another Anglo-Saxon feature of modern villages: the green. In the days when ravenous wolves roamed the forests, it was a good idea to have a large enclosure where domestic animals could graze and still be safe from predators. Often, this enclosure would contain a pond and be surrounded by the houses of the village. In time this convenient stretch of grass was used for games and fairs; the village green was born. Another important step made by the Anglo-Saxons was the brewing of barley into beer, and the construction of inns where it could be drunk.

It should not be thought that our Anglo-Saxon heritage in the village ends there, however. Many of the names by which places are known date back to the dark days when farmers tried to avoid the roaming bands of warriors. It is often interesting to take the name of a local place and decipher its origins, particularly as some names refer to ancient words that have long since disappeared from the English language.

One of the most important of these is the -ing ending. This can usually be translated as 'followers of' or 'tribe of'. Hastings, for example, was settled by the followers of a lord called Haesta. Another very common ending is -ley, -ly or -leigh, all of which derive from the Anglo-Saxon word leah. This word meant a clearing in a forest, so a group of villages whose names end in - ley is a good indication that an area was once covered by dense forest. Likewise, any place name ending in -well can be taken to be the site of a spring.

Just as the Anglo-Saxons were getting their lifestyle sorted out, with a profusion of villages and a few market towns, the whole of society reeled under a sudden onslaught. Fierce, pagan barbarians threw themselves at the country. Land was laid waste and whole communities slaughtered. The Vikings had arrived.

Eventually the Vikings were defeated, but many of them settled down and left a mark on the land that cannot be ignored. Isolated farms had far more appeal to the new settlers than to the native Anglo-Saxons; a tendency that is still noticeable in what was once the Danelaw. The place names of an area will often reveal much about its Scandinavian past. Villages whose names end in -by began life as individual Viking farms, while thorp means an outlying settlement near a larger community. Other Scandinavian words survive in place names; words such as bekk meaning stream, melr meaning sand and thveit meaning forest clearing.

Seven centuries ago the pattern of agriculture was very different from that of today. The land surrounding a village was divided up into three great fields and each of these was split into a series of strips which were distributed amongst the villagers. The path that was beaten to a village tended to be straight for a furlong, then turn at right angles to run along the top of a strip before turning another right angle and continuing on its way. When the strip system of agriculture broke up, the roads remained. Today, the path winding past the strip fields has become the sudden double-bend which is such an irritation to motorists.

So though few actual buildings in a village will date back more than a few centuries, its layout and form are descended from the earliest days of English settlement and owe much to trades and violence now long vanished.

Nestling in the rolling Dorset hills, Cerne Abbas (top) is perhaps the archetypal vision of the English village, its well-balanced growth of buildings showing how a compact community, surrounded by farmland, has clustered around its 15th-century church. A village green provides the central focus at Finchingfield in Essex (right), but again the church is the dominant feature. To visitors and locals alike, nothing is more restful than a spring morning's contemplative wander through a magnolia-shaded village churchyard dotted with gravestones ancient and modern, as at Overbury (above).

With the decline of milling, preserving existing mill-houses (previous pages) became an important part of village heritage: Hambledon Mill, Buckinghamshire (left) and Houghton Mill in the Cambridgeshire Fens (right) lend backwater serenity to the bustle of village centres. Equally serene on dry land are the Jacobean arches (right) of Chipping Campden's Market Hall, Gloucestershire while these earlier cottages – at Bridge End, Warwick (above) and Anne Hathaway's house (centre), near Stratford-upon-Avon possess a timeless charm which the Victorians tried to emulate at Horning, by the River Bure in Norfolk (top).

For all the inconvenience it causes, there is nothing like a moderate fall of snow to sharpen the perception of line and form (previous pages), smoothing, for instance, the church roof at Earl's Colne near Colchester to emphasise the cobbled surface of its flint walls, and highlighting the ornate dormers of Priory's Croft at Dorney in Berkshire. Soft sunlight enhances the colour and tone of single dwellings, as (above) at Ibsley in Hampshire; of entire villages, as (top) at Salcombe in Devon; and especially of picturesque harbours, of which Cornwall's Polperro (right) is a striking example.

Previous pages: 16th-century town houses in Canterbury's Westgate (left) lose a little of their original character for the sake of smartness. Compare the birthplace of Thomas Hardy (right) at Higher Bockhampton in Dorset, which retains its old rusticity. These pages: villages for recreation; (top) summer cricket in the New Forest; (above left) narrowboat leisure at Tiverton, Devon; (right) visitors enjoy the peace of Castle Combe in Wiltshire; (above right) an unusual two-storey Herefordshire farm building. Overleaf: villages for sailing enthusiasts: Brixham's quayside (left) boasts various craft, while Clovelly's harbour (right) attracts more solitary sailing.

Much of the attraction of English villages lies in their secluded locations. The remoteness of Widecombe-in-the-Moor (top) is emphasised by the long road winding over Dartmoor to link it to larger towns. Brick cottages (above), formerly shipwrights' houses, offer unexpected delights at Buckler's Hard, Hampshire, while Anne Hathaway's cottage (right), dating in part from the 1400s, lies a good mile outside Stratford. Overleaf: towers and spires dominate at Ledbury, Herefordshire (left), where the Georgian spire of St Michael and All Angels, set on a medieval tower, almost menaces the prettily decorated Church Street, and at Corfe Castle (right), whose crumbling ruins still impose a gaunt authority over the Purbeck village below.

A lily-covered pond, a modest, medieval-towered church, and a tile-hung cottage make Chiddingfold (top) a handsome Surrey village. Broader waters give a feeling of spaciousness to Christchurch, whose elegantly-proportioned priory (right) is seen across the River Stour in Hampshire. Above: in Rye, Sussex, a sloping, cobbled street lined with period houses takes the visitor on a journey back in time. Broadway, in Worcestershire (overleaf), has more period uniformity, with its uphill rows of warm, Cotswold stone cottages, relentlessly terraced, yet tantalisingly individual in height, width and depth, roofline and frontage.

The Industrial Revolution spawned many new villages in the Midlands and the north-west of England, where the incidence of moor and fell has combined to offer a distinctive regional attraction. Matlock Bath (left), on the Derwent, is typical of several villages east of Manchester, with river, road and hillside community indicating brisk wealth in a bygone age. By contrast, the Gloucestershire village of Chipping Campden (top) sports an expansive gatehouse and the fine, honey-coloured tower of St James's Church, lending an air of more serene prosperity. For today's well-to-do, a renovated cottage, such as this one (above), set in a lush garden deep in Hampshire, is a much sought-after reward for life's work.

Trimly thatched and pink-washed, the Elizabethan cottages at Cavendish, Suffolk (previous pages, left), where colourful exterior shades are a speciality, are a local showpiece. The castellated St Mary's Church mirrors their rosy glow in its stonework and knapped-flint towers. Nature's warmest pink is seen (previous pages, right) in rhododendrons flourishing in a Surrey graveyard – that of the tiny village church at Oakwood Hill. In the north of England, the hamlet of Muker huddles in the immensity of the Yorkshire Dales (top), while the north-east coast port of Whitby (left), with its fascinating old church and spectacular abbey ruins, boasts history, beache and incomparable maritime charm. The wool trade enabled East Anglia and Kent to thrive. The Swan Inn at Lavenham, Suffolk (above) is just one of many 15th-century merchants' houses, as is the boldly-proportioned house (overleaf right) at Headcorn, Kent. Iron-forging brought wealth to Surrey's Abinger Hammer (overleaf, left), so called because the swift current of its stream powered a forge-hammer in Tudor times. A more modern clock, with its hammer-struck chimes, recalls those prosperous days.

A pale sun on weathered stone justifies the name of Gold Hill, in Shaftesbury (left), whose curling line of artisans' houses seems to lean against an inexorable gradient. The steep banks of the River Nidd give Yorkshire's Knaresborough (above) a similarly terraced, if more broadly based, look. The quiet, much more gently situated village of Alfold in Surrey (top) counts a small Norman church as its main attraction

Previous pages: two rural gems from Gloucestershire; a well preserved early Victorian mill and mill-house at Lower Slaughter (left), and the attractive garden of a riverside house at Naunton. On the south coast, the splendid little fishing village of Bosham (top), part of Chichester Harbour, is a haven for shore birds, while its riverfront buildings, dominated by the Saxon church beyond, produce an arresting visual effect. Rather more dramatic is the approach to Clovelly Harbour in Devon (left) – an irresistible challenge to tourists and delight to the eye of the connoisseur of colour, perspective and shifting vistas. Three Airs Cottage (above left) is one of few pre-Georgian buildings left at Wareham in Dorset, a village largely destroyed by fire in 1762. Further east lies the yachting centre of Lymington, whose narrow streets, like Nelson Place (above right), slope down to the estuary and the Solent. Overleaf: these Herefordshire cottages – one late medieval and thatched, the other Victorian and slate-roofed – have been beautifully set off by a profusion of floral colour.

An end view (above) of the cottage on the previous page, shows the thorough beam-work which its 15th-century builders put into its construction. The chimney, slightly out of character, is probably a much later addition. At Wareham (top), the early 19th-century building has remained, but with a change of use: the restaurant's name recalls its previous trade, as does the name of the bookshop in Lavenham's Water Street (right): note again the preference for exterior colour-washes, and the years of careful preservation of timbered properties further up the street. Overleaf: English naval traditions die hard. Masts clutter the harbour at Yarmouth, Isle of Wight (left), while on the mainland, residents of the hill village of Kingswear (right) can watch craft of all shapes and sizes plying the River Dart. The bank in the foreground is part of Dartmouth.

A pleasant, unassuming parish church among a profusion of ancient, timber-framed, flower-banked cottages characterises the unspoilt village of Welford-upon-Avon (left). The river skirts the village on three sides to give other, equally attractive views. Water has its place at Upper Slaughter (top) through which the clear, blue River Eye runs, and had a purpose at Farningham in Kent, where this fine old mill-house (above) is splendidly preserved. More powerfully, the Thames passes through the picture-postcard village of Goring, on the Berkshire/Oxfordshire borders (overleaf left), and requires a lock to regulate water-levels. No such problems at Kersey, Suffolk (overleaf right), however, where the main road can usually be forded with ease.

An ever-widening River Exe flows past houses and cottages at Bickleigh in Devon (top), on its way to Lyme Bay at Exeter. More immediate coastal approaches have different, though still picturesque qualities, such as the Sinnock Square quarter of Hastings, Sussex (above left) and Quay Hill (right), which connects Lymington's High Street with the sea. A fresh coat of scarlet paint distinguishes this crisply-decorated, late Georgian building in Wimborne Minster, Dorset (above right), where no fewer than seven roads meet to link town, country and coast. Overleaf: Gloucestershire attractions in town and village. Tewkesbury's Jacobean riverside dwellings (left) comprise only a small proportion of dozens of timbered houses and hostelries, while the expansive and ornate 12th-century tower of the Abbey reaffirms the town's august and ancient origins. Less ancient – by some 600 years – is the terrace of mill buildings (right) in Sherborne Street, Bourton-on-the-Water.

The village of Buckland (top) in Surrey compactly contains tiny parish church, old village green and round pond all within the same easy view. Midhurst (right); in neighbouring Sussex, spreads much more freely, several streets lying between a broad, irregular lake and a venerable old church. Both Midhurst and Rye (above right) minted their own trading tokens as currency in Tudor days. Their chief trade was in wool, as also at Cranbrook in Kent (above left), where an octagonal, still operative, 19th-century windmill testifies to the importance of clothmaking industries. Overleaf: a many-windowed thatched cottage (left) at Hanley Castle, Worcestershire; and the welcoming sight of the Bell Inn (right) at Hurley-on-Thames in Berkshire.

Brixham Harbour (right) is typical of a community capable of retaining some attraction despite its necessarily close-packed layout. Far away, however, from the busy centres of commerce or recreation, English villages are able to progress in an unhurried, sometimes isolated manner. Even at the roadside, Holland House (top) at Cropthorne rambles in its own defined, if somewhat restricted grounds in Worcestershire, while the Herefordshire cottage (above) breathes easily in its pretty garden. Despite the need for constant repair, medieval houses like Priest's House (overleaf left), in the Surrey village of Leigh, continue to flourish in peace, while the Tudor Peacock tea-rooms at Chilham, Kent (overleaf right) remind us that, centuries ago, pilgrims stopped here for refreshment on their way to and from Canterbury. It is good to know that England's villages can prosper without becoming mere museum pieces. Following page: Bickleigh in Devon.